Elias Hill
101 Engineer Jokes For Engineers
Copyright 2017
Self-published, Tiny Camel Books

Tiny Camel Books
tinycamelbooks.com
tinycamelbooks@gmail.com

101
Engineer Jokes
For Engineers

By: Elias Hill

Illustrations By: Katherine Hogan

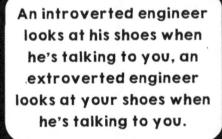

What's the difference between an introverted and an extroverted engineer?

An introverted engineer looks at his shoes when he's talking to you, an extroverted engineer looks at your shoes when he's talking to you.

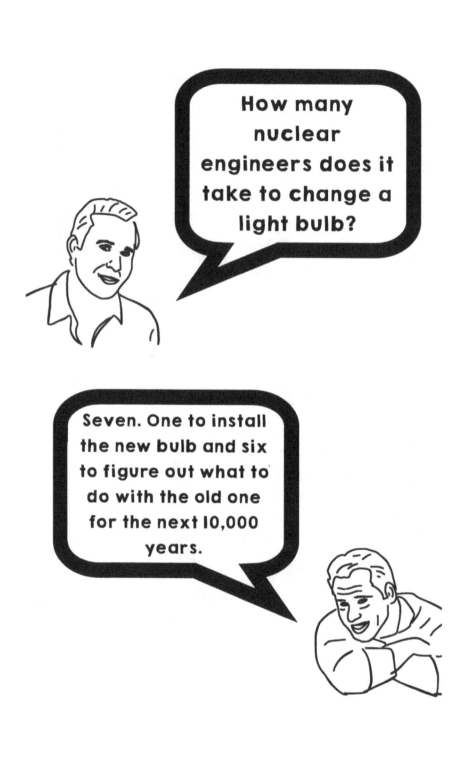

A physicist and an engineer were given a red rubber ball and told to find the volume.

The physicist filled a beaker with water, put the ball in the water, and measured the total displacement.

The engineer looked up the model and serial numbers in his red-rubber-ball table.

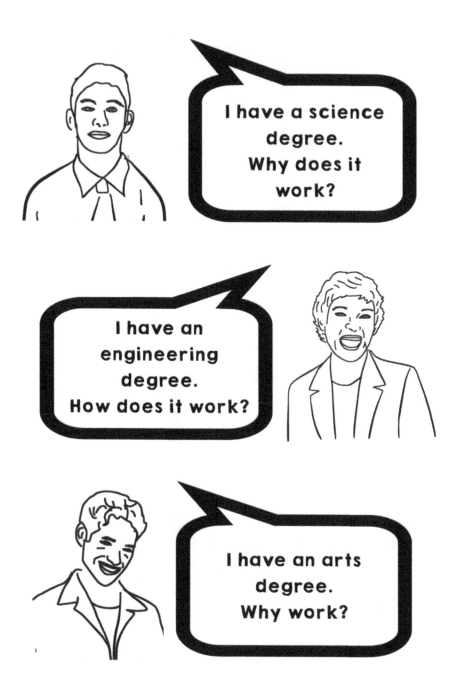

Please conserve energy and turn off all lights.

Ha, jokes on you, energy is always conserved.

Two antennas met on a roof, fell in love and got married.

The ceremony wasn't much, but the reception was excellent.

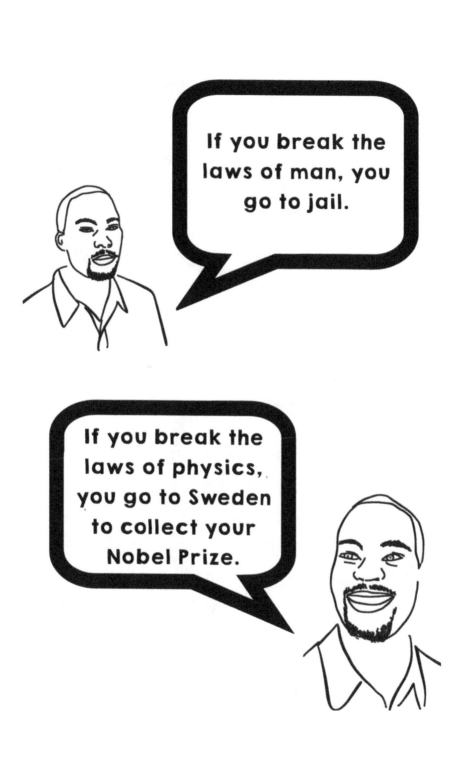

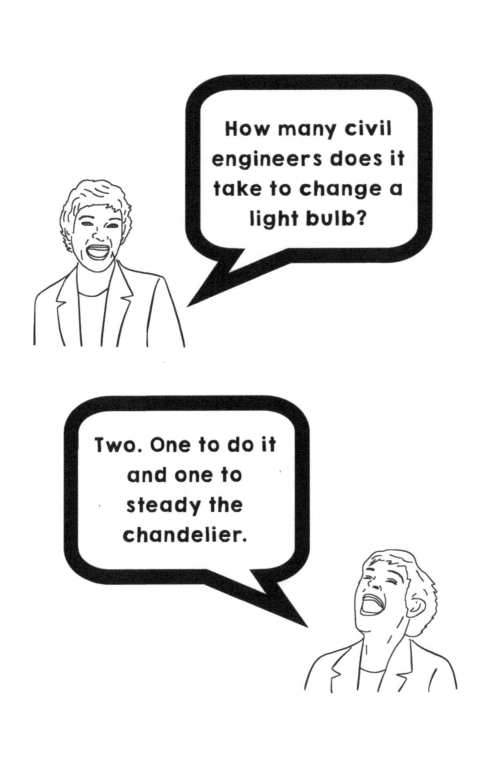

Why shouldn't computer engineers be surgeons?
Because they would just turn off all the body functions and start them up again.

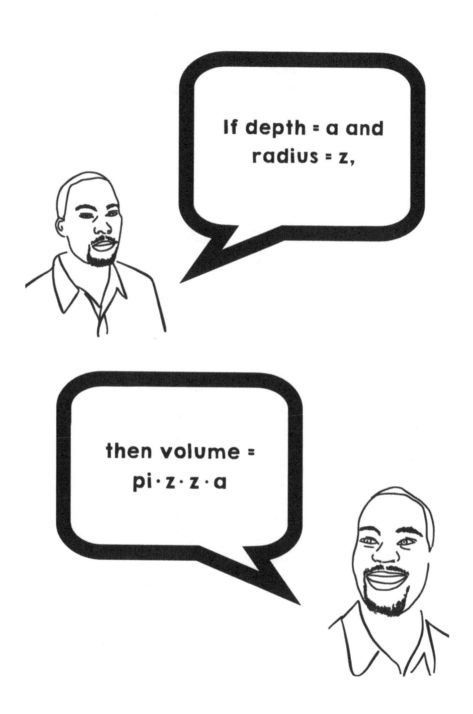

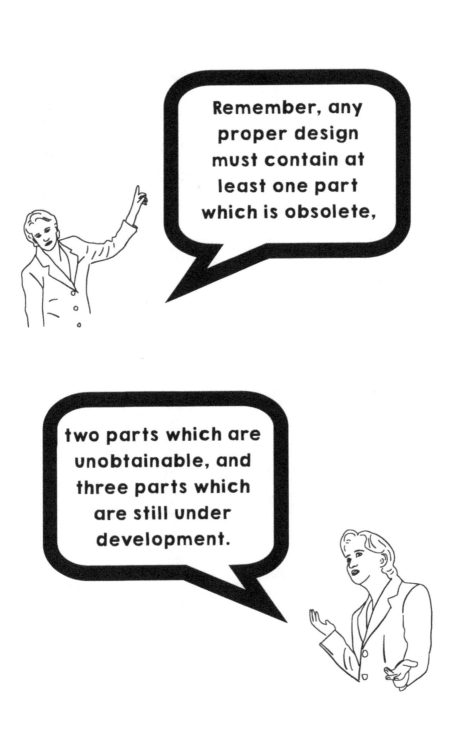

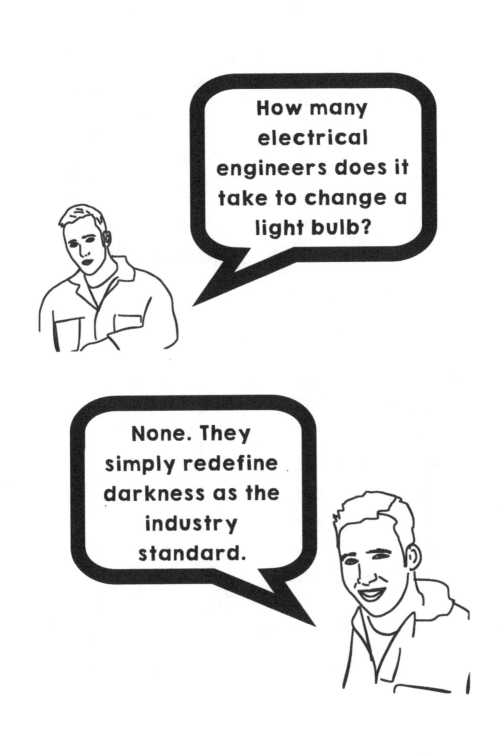

You might be an engineer if...

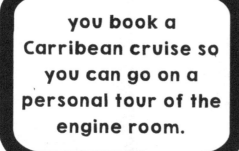

you book a Carribean cruise so you can go on a personal tour of the engine room.

Hey, nice bike! Where did you get it?

I was walking to math class the other day when this hot coed rides up on this bike. She jumps off, takes off her clothes, and says, "You can have anything you want!"

Good choice, her clothes wouldn't have fit you anyway.

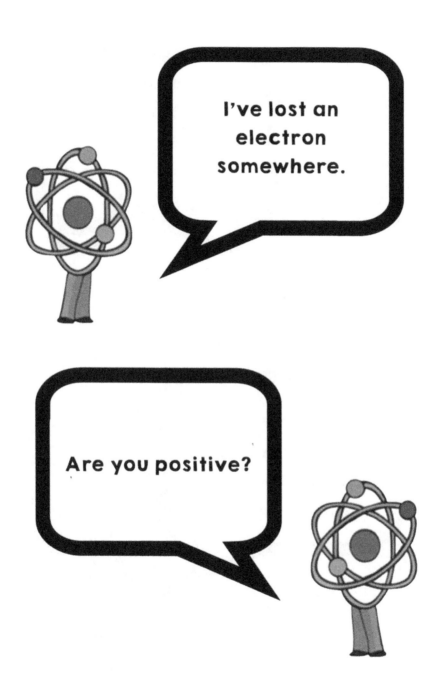

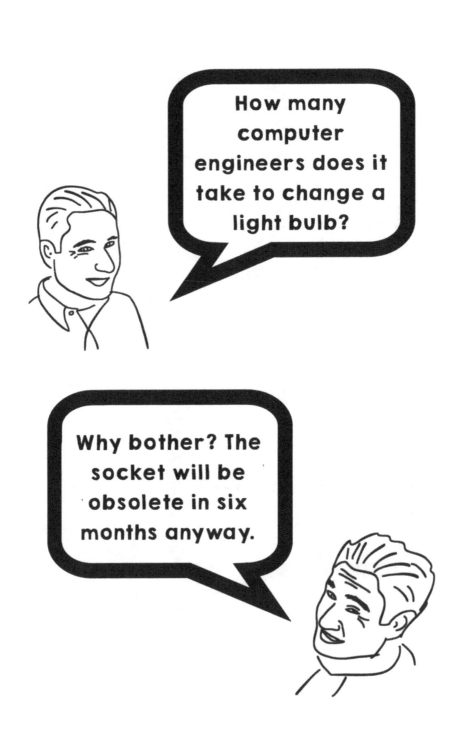

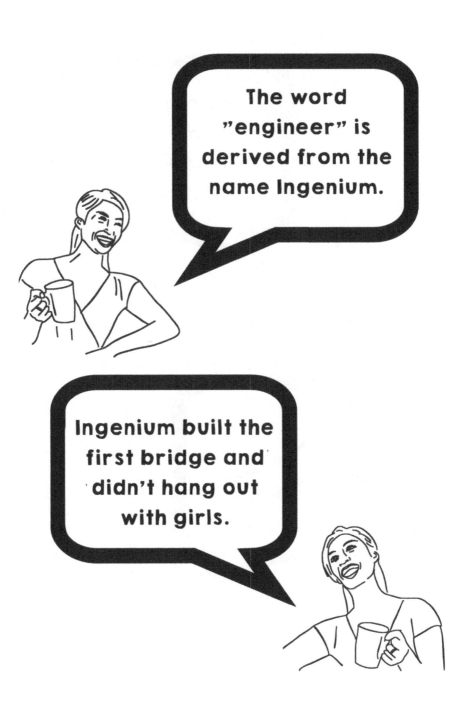

Arguing with an engineer is like wrestling with a pig in the mud.
After few minutes you realize the pig likes it.

How many mechanical engineers does it take to change a light bulb?

Five. One to decide which way the bulb ought to turn, one to calculate the force required, one to design a tool with which to turn the bulb, one to design a comfortable, but functional, hand grip, and one to use all this equipment.

Made in the USA
Las Vegas, NV
14 March 2021